For Tara
with love
V. F.

Printed and bound in Singapore by Tien Wah Press (PTE) Ltd.

First U.S. edition   1 2 3 4 5 6 7 8 9 10

Library of Congress Cataloging in Publication Data
French, Vivian. One ballerina two / written by Vivian French ; illustrated by Jan Ormerod.
    p.   cm.   Summary: Two young ballerinas practice their steps and movements.
ISBN 0-688-10333-2. — ISBN 0-688-10334-0 (lib. bdg.)   1. Ballet—Pictorial works—Juvenile
literature.   2. Ballerinas—Pictorial works—Juvenile literature.   [1. Ballet dancing.
2. Counting.]   I. Ormerod, Jan, ill.   II. Title.   III. Title: 1 ballerina 2.   GV1787.5.F7
1991   792.8022'2—dc20   [E]
90-45969 CIP AC

One Ballerina Two

Written by Vivian French   Illustrated by Jan Ormerod

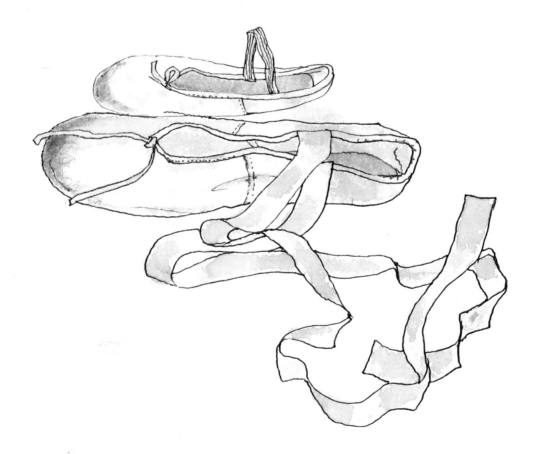

Lothrop, Lee & Shepard Books
New York

Ballerinas…

us two

10 Ten pliés

9   Nine knee bends

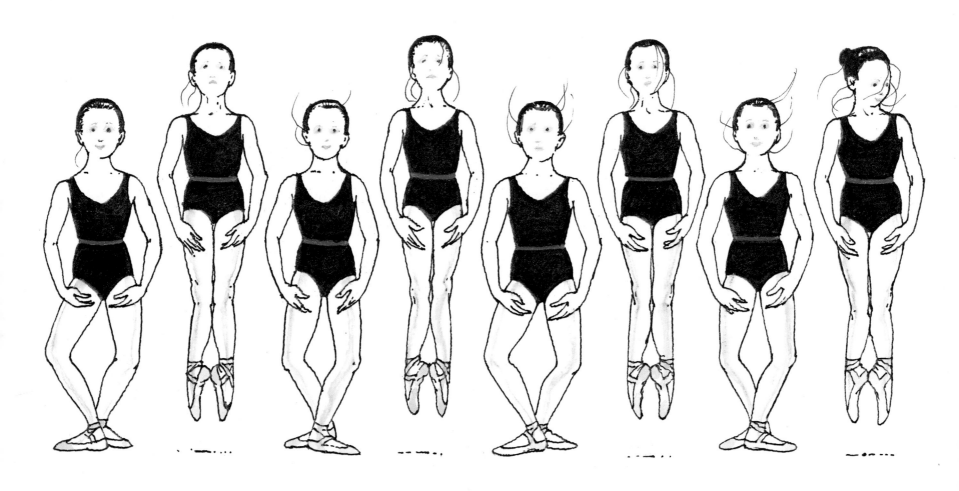

8 Eight changements

7. Seven little jumps

6 Six pirouettes

5 Five gallops

oops!

4 Four pas de chat

3 Three pony trots

2 Two final curtsies

One happy hug